Y0-DBX-823

Effective Parenting! Capable Kids!

By Rosemarie Pérez, Karen Salzer, Ph.D., Carole Flowers, and Mary Ann Burke, ·Ed.D.

Effective Parenting! Capable Kids! Copyright © 2017 by Rosemarie Pérez, Karen Salzer, Ph.D., Carole Flowers, and Mary Ann Burke, Ed.D. All rights reserved. Published by Novation Associates, San Jose, CA. No portion of this book may be reproduced, stored in a retrieval system, or transmitted in any form or by any means, mechanical, electronic, photocopying, recording, or otherwise without written permission from the publisher. For more information regarding permission, email hello@genparenting.com.

Cover Artwork by Nancy Perez

Library of Congress Control Number: 2017904780
CreateSpace Independent Publishing Platform, North Charleston, SC

ISBN-13: 978-1544039169
ISBN-10: 1544039166

DEDICATION

This book is dedicated to the many families who have shared their stories through the GenParenting.com blog and at various parent trainings.

CONTENTS

ACKNOWLEDGMENTS

Parents continually provide us with heartwarming stories about how they have overcome daily challenges with their children. ***Effective Parenting! Capable Kids!*** was created from parents' stories of successes and challenges shared on the GenParenting.com blog and from the parent trainings we have conducted during the past thirty years.

As credentialed teachers, educational trainers, parents, and active grandmothers, we regularly care for our grandchildren as well as support our communities' schools. Our work with families has been through school programs where we have been able to personally help parents through parent education classes. We have conducted academic enrichment workshops and demonstrated how children can learn while engaged in a playful activity.

We wish to thank our families who have spent countless hours supporting our work by providing feedback and support as we developed our GenParenting.com blog. We wish to thank Laura Rinaldi, our graphic designer and website coach, for the technical support she has provided our team while we learned how to manage our blogging and publication needs. We acknowledge the leadership that Chrissy Watson provided our team in developing our branding and marketing strategies. A special thanks to Michele McDevitt, Bruce Wiener, and Pilar Borvice for their editorial support in completing our final draft of this book. Finally, we want to thank the many educators and families who have shared their student and family experiences. Without their support and guidance, this book could not have been created.

This book is designed to support culturally diverse parents of newborn through secondary school age children in developing effective parenting skills and literacy/academic play activities. For added support, log onto the GenParenting.com website at http://www.genparenting.com. Weekly blogs focus on parenting, family health, special needs, and resources. Added feedback and guidance is provided by emailing us at hello@genparenting.com.

CHAPTER 1
EFFECTIVELY COMMUNICATE
WITH YOUR CHILDREN

The key ingredient to a gratifying relationship with our children is effective communication. As families, we communicate for many reasons and in many different ways. We communicate when we play and enjoy each other's company. We converse about experiences, beliefs and opinions we hold. We discuss decisions we have to make or problems we need to solve. Sometimes as parents we provide discipline. A look or a nod may be all our children need in order to know that we are tuned in to what they are doing. Whether it is a nod of approval for a great accomplishment or a look of disapproval for a poor behavior choice, being there and paying attention to our children communicates love and caring. Effective communication starts with being attentive and ready to listen to what our children have to say, no matter their age or stage of development.

Listening is the most important part of communicating because through listening, we learn what our children need and how best to respond. When we listen, sometimes it's necessary to repeat what our children are saying or to rephrase what we are hearing to make sure we are getting the story straight. We listen for how they are feeling so that we can put ourselves in their shoes and better understand what they need from us. When our children tell us things that disappoint us or require that we discipline them, we can still be empathetic and understand their thinking. If we are empathetic, our communication will show our love for our children, even when we are providing discipline. As we continue to communicate over time, we will become more skilled at choosing the right words, the most effective tone of voice, and body language so that our messages will be clearly understood.

Whether the purpose of our communication is casual or serious, if we establish an attitude of mutual respect in our communication, many conflicts will be averted. Communicating with mutual respect can allow us to express differing opinions without having to revert to arguments or fighting. We or our children may not always be happy at the end of some conversations. With a respectful approach, we will have a better chance of coming to agreement and finding solutions to problems.

As I have become a better listener, my responses have been more welcomed by my family members, even when the messages have not been positive ones. Of course, I am not perfect when I slip into my old habits of reacting before listening or raising my voice, I see the difference in the reactions I receive from my family. Effective communication deepens our relationships with our loved ones. Those are the bonds that last over time.

How to Use "I Messages"

Back in the 1980's I learned about "I Messages." I was taught that when communicating with someone about something that bothers me, instead of laying blame, it was more effective to speak about how it made me feel. So instead of saying, "You are always so rude to me!" I could instead say, "I feel hurt when you speak rudely to me." I was pleasantly surprised when I began giving parenting workshops that the curriculum made use of these "I messages" in progressive ways.

One of the ways we can reinforce positive behavior in our children is to recognize the good behavioral decisions they make. We can do this through an "I love you" message. An example would be "I love you very much. I see that you came home and began doing your homework before I had to remind you. I feel proud when I see you

2

becoming more responsible." We begin our communication by telling our children we love them. We also express our feelings about their positive behavior. Our children love to receive positive feedback from us when it is real and specific.

When our children make poor behavior decisions, this "I love you" message can be equally as effective. When we need to discipline our children, it is helpful for them to understand that discipline flows from love. It can sound like, "You know that I love you very much. I was disappointed to hear that you have not been handing in your homework. Why is this happening?" Framing the conversation this way provides a better opportunity for more productive responses from our children. They realize we are concerned because we love them. This also helps them understand our feelings about the situation. Speaking from love also helps keep our emotions in check while we get to the bottom of what's going on.

Everything we do or say provides examples for our children to follow. When we speak from love and communicate from the perspective of how we feel, our children will learn to do the same. Over time, these communication patterns will profoundly change the way we talk to each other at home. They will also affect how our children will communicate outside of the home with their peers and other adults, and support effective problem-solving at school.

Sometimes we just need to take a deep breath and remember why we are parents. When we do that, the love will flow and our communication will be more effective.

When Should You Communicate with Our Children?

Frustrated parents tell me they have little time to have long meaningful conversations with their children. There is work in and out of the home. Children have activities they must complete each day. We all lead very busy lives.

I'm reminded of the times I used to spend with my father. He was a very busy contractor. He worked all the time. But, since he didn't have a son, he chose me to be his helper. I would hold the lamp over the engines of his vehicles as he repaired them. I would hand him the proper tools or help put on a fresh coat of paint in order to keep his equipment in working order. During those times, we would talk. I learned of his past and dreams for the future. He would tell me of the dreams he had for me, the qualities he saw in me and the reasons why he wanted me to be educated. We discussed family, current events and many other things that I can no longer remember. I do remember how this time was special to me and to him. It was our time to connect.

Talking with our children does not always need to be a planned event. We can talk while we clean up after dinner, while we drive together in the car, while we pull weeds and work in the backyard. Whatever tasks we need to complete around the house, we can do them with our children and use this time to talk.

Parents have told me they take their older kids with them when they go for a walk or to the gym. They shut off the television once in a while and play board games. They go out for pizza or ice cream to celebrate after the family completes a major chore like cleaning the garage.

Everyday living gives us opportunities to work and play together. The conversations that occur during these informal times may well be the conversations that will be most remembered. Most importantly, during these times we get to know each other better and deepen our relationships with our children. This will prepare us for the times when problems occur and communication will be the most critical. Having built closeness during the informal times, we will have built the foundation for the understanding and trust that will make communication more effective when times get tough. Enjoy times of work and play together as often as you can.

How to Increase Communication

What is your quality time with your children when it is cold outside and they are tired of playing alone? Do you respond to your children's boredom by turning on the television or using the smart phone for entertainment? Many parents are so busy with their daily responsibilities that they may only talk or play with their children less than twenty minutes per day. Some parents do not see their children during the work week due to long commutes. Working parents may only have weekends available to play with their children. Solutions to the limited time available for quality time with your children include the following:

- For one week, track the number of minutes you were able to talk, play, or read to your children each day.
- Be conscious of how you can increase the communication time with your children through phone calls or video chats using a smart phone or computer.
- Consider how you can adjust your schedule and errands to maximize your time with your children.
- During meal times focus your attention on individual family members. Engage each member in conversation.
- Read a story to your children and have them discuss the story with you.
- At bedtime, spend fifteen minutes with each child. Do not judge when the child reflects on the day's events.
- Ask your child to tell you one good thing that happened at school and one thing that did not work out. Ask your child about their response to the challenging situation.
- As the child shares the daily activities, the parent can share daily challenges and successes.

As you share your daily reflections with each other, remind your children that tomorrow is a new day and they can shape it into whatever they want for the day. Use quality time with your children to stay informed of their experiences.

CHAPTER 2
RESOLVE CONFLICTS
WITH YOUR CHILDREN

Due to the demands of managing a home and working outside the home, most parents have little time to reflect on life and the daily challenges of raising their children. At best, parents may have a passing moment to share their frustrations with a partner, a family member, or a friend. Parents typically share with us that they limit conflicts with their children by giving into their child's demands in public. Sadly, this response to their child only reinforces misbehaviors without boundaries or consequences. Children quickly learn that boundaries can be broken. Children can continually push the limits to seek more privileges without appropriate consequences until their lives and their parents' responses are out of control.

Conflicts in families can occur at any time. Sometimes we can plan ahead to reward positive behaviors and limit conflict. Effective conflict management strategies include creating a behavioral rewards chart that lists behaviors which have previously led to conflict. This chart should have a place to record positive behavior with a star, happy face, sticker, or checkmark. When our children were young, taking baths, picking up toys, and brushing teeth were chronic sources of conflict. I made up a chart listing four or five of these daily activities with a place for stars for successful completion. An agreed upon number of stars might mean that a child earns a reward such as a Happy Meal from McDonald's, a movie outing with mom, or a play date with dad.

When teaching in my classroom, I had a weekly raffle of gift certificates or items donated by local merchants. I awarded tickets for task completion, packing up on time, or staying on task. I had a list of the behaviors that I was looking for posted in the classroom. Every Friday, I would pick a random raffle ticket and give out a prize. On Monday, I would start over with an empty container for raffle tickets and a fresh start.

To minimize conflicts at home, I used an old-fashioned egg timer, kitchen timer, or phone timer to set how much time was allotted for a behavior such as completing homework, getting dressed for school, or picking up toys. Remember that these are just tools for you to use whenever you can prevent a power struggle.

Reduce Conflicts During Power Struggles

How do you manage conflict when you are in the middle of a power struggle with your child? Examples may include:

- You are out grocery shopping with your three year old who starts crying for the candy strategically located at the checkout line.
- Your teenager has just passed the driving test and wants to drive, but you need your car.
- Your middle schooler has broken curfew and not contacted you.

Once the struggle has begun, how can you change direction? The first thing you have to do is calm down. Second, help your child to calm down. Third, move on. Here are some strategies for doing this:

- Take away the audience. Defusing conflict requires focus, privacy, and quiet. Find a quiet place, such as the child's bedroom, where you can talk to your child alone.
- Use timeouts. Find a change of setting to get away from the situation, such as a walk outside, or some time alone. These actions can help you and your child to remain calm.

- Use incentives to change behavior. An incentive such as food, the promise of a play date, or even television time can be negotiated to reframe the conflict.
- Minimize time in a power struggle.
- Be straightforward and remember that the word "No" can be a complete sentence. End the discussion and move on to talking about happy times ahead.

Once, when our three year old granddaughter was far away from home, she was unable to stop crying. Her mother placed a chair for her to sit on in a peaceful outside setting within mom's view. It was designated as the crying chair. Time sitting on this chair was not punitive, but a constructive opportunity to decompress. It was a very effective strategy.

One of my most difficult teacher-student situations occurred when a high school student started to cut her hair in front of all of us and waved the scissors at us as we approached. I took her on a walk to a calming pathway near the high school that was on the way to her home. I had disengaged from trying to get the scissors away from her. She voluntarily put them down at the mention of going home. Things calmed down enough that I was able to walk back to school with her, call her mother, and have her picked up. Every day we are faced with the potential for conflict with our children regardless of how old they are. We should remain focused on responding directly, staying calm, and remembering our unbiased love and affection for them.

Use Timeouts to Reduce Sibling Conflicts

How many times have felt you were losing your mind when your kids fight? Many times I have found myself regularly trying to keep the peace only to have the children fight me in the process. One day, I finally changed my approach. I told the children that when they fight or hurt each other, all of them would have to take a timeout! The children resisted. They could not understand why they would be punished if they did not start the conflict. They complained that I was not being fair. Then they challenged my ability to take the time to understand the conflict and make a judgement about who was right and who was wrong.

What I learned from these situations was that no one is innocent in a conflict. Everyone has a role in the conflict. Some children were the bullies while others resisted the conflict and acted as victims. My solution was simple. I established zero-tolerance for conflict in our home. Some days were great! The kids played cooperatively together with little conflict. Other days were spent with a couple of timeouts for all children.

Although the approach seemed harsh, my adult children are the best of friends. I apply these parenting strategies with my grandchildren. The results are similar with less conflict. I also remind my older grandchildren that I am not taking the time to care for them just to watch them fight. That is on their time. My time is best spent with fun days of play and adventures.

Set Boundaries for Misbehavior in Public

Summarized below are five effective strategies for managing your children's misbehavior in grocery stores and other public places:

- When in the car or preparing for an outing, explain the types of cooperative behavior you expect from you children. For example, you can tell them that they must only handle groceries which you have selected or which they can select with your guidance. Decide whether they can sit in the shopping cart or walk next to you in the store. For older children, you can describe how they can select fruits and vegetables on your shopping list, evaluate the quality of the produce, weigh each selection, and calculate and predict the cost of specific selections. This may sound like a lot of work on your part, but this activity can be a cooperative learning experience that reinforces every day problem-solving using real world math applications.
- When discussing misbehavior, you and your children can agree to a logical consequence that will occur if they do not cooperate. For example, children may need to leave the store

with you immediately when they choose to have temper tantrums. This may seem like a punishment to you and not your children, but all must regroup in excessive situations. The children will soon learn that they cannot participate in outings with you if they are not cooperative. Other logical consequences for minor misbehaviors can include rewarding cooperative behaviors. You can inform your children that if they cooperate with you on an outing, you will have time to play a game with them once you unload groceries or unpack the car. The children will quickly learn that there is always time for more fun when the family cooperates and works together.

- After you complete your shopping or outing, reflect with your children on what went right and how you can work more closely together for success. For example, you can comment on how cooperative your children were when keeping their hands to themselves even when they wanted a food item at the store that was not selected by you. You can also explain that they may not select specific food items the next time you shop because they chose to pull food items off the shelf that were not on your shopping list.

- After the outing, assure your children that you appreciate their cooperative behavior. If they have misbehaved, tell them they can have another chance to cooperate and participate in selecting items during the next shopping trip.

- Limit the discussion to simplify the communication and consequences. Your children will not hear you while they are misbehaving or when you are feeling overwhelmed and continue talking about the problem.

Strengthen Parent-Child Relationships Through Dialogue

We set enormous expectations for our families during the holidays. These expectations may have led to some angry discussions at the family events. Our children take their cues on how to behave when they watch us. Also, our kids may have felt pressure because we required their "best behavior" at these family events. One of the first places where our children learn about conflict is in their family. How can such conflict strengthen parent-child relationships? When you and your child have had a power struggle, take time to talk about what has happened with the following guidelines:

- Clarify your expectations and explain how they were not met.
- Allow time for each person to speak without interruption.
- Set the timer for three minutes per person until each person has presented their own side.
- Come to a mutual agreement about how the rules will be followed in the future.
- Above all, remember how precious your children are.
- Love and respect these precious times together.

I applied these strategies in my own life when my children fought over who would ride shotgun in my car. They might yell "shotgun" or run and climb into the front seat. They might wrestle with each other. It was a seemingly unresolvable conflict in which someone always felt cheated. This happened over and over again.

One day when we were all calm, I asked them to come up with a solution that would be fair to everyone. They agreed that they would take turns. Because they each had a voice in the decision, there was less conflict over this issue in the future. This helped everyone practice resolving conflict in a respectful manner.

Become Role Models for Your Teens

It is never too late to adjust your parenting style. Positive results may take longer to achieve, but will lead to better outcomes. We are role models for our teens. Teens observe how we deal with problems. They adopt the attitudes we demonstrate and the actions we take to cope with problems. We need to be aware of what we are teaching our teens through our example. Here is a process for problem solving that may serve as a guide for parents:

- Listen without interruption to your teen as they describe the problem.
- Listen for how your teen is feeling about the situation.

- Ask questions and make suggestions to develop options for solving the problem.
- Ask questions and make suggestions to determine the consequences that may result from taking each option.
- Offer encouragement and support for the option your teen decides to take.
- Follow up to see how it went and to offer further support.

Our teens need our guidance as they navigate the challenges that come up in their lives. We can show them through our example that problems are temporary. We can guide them through the process and be there to provide emotional support. Eventually, our teens will be able to problem-solve for themselves as they move towards adulthood.

How to Problem-Solve with Your Teens

Our teens want to go out with friends. Do we let them go, or not? How will we know that they will be safe? What are the factors we need to consider?

I work a lot with immigrant parents, grandparents and guardians. Often parents decide that the way to keep their children safe is to withhold permission and to keep them at home. Many immigrant and first generation parents were raised around an extended family that provided safety, nurturing and entertainment to the children as they grew up. Although these parents may no longer live in those extended family environments, many feel that restricting their children's independence is the only way to protect them.

Adolescence is the time when children should develop independence from their parents. In preparation for adulthood, preteens and teens must learn to make responsible decisions when their parents are not around. Denying teenagers and even preteens a level of independence puts them at a disadvantage later in life. If not prepared, they will have to experience the consequences of poor decision-making when they are adults. Yet, giving them too much independence before they are ready can have disastrous results as well.

Often teens, especially those who live in restrictive homes, find ways to work around their parent's restrictions either by lying or sneaking out. This puts parents at a disadvantage because they don't know where their children are and have not had the opportunity to prepare them for what they may face. These teens or preteens are out in the world without the needed direction and guidance. Worst of all, the relationship of trust between parents and children is lost when lying becomes common practice. Although it is a challenge, guiding our children to be independent and establishing consequences for positive and negative decisions can be a more effective way to prepare our children for adulthood.

We set the foundation for providing this guidance by being engaged in our children's interests and activities when they are young. When we are involved at school, with their sports teams and their hobbies, we create opportunities to be with them in their social world. Our relationships with our kids are strengthened when we know their friends and their friends' families. When the time comes that they ask us for permission to go out, we will have more knowledge on which to base our decision.

Here are some questions that can guide us as we consider whether to let them go out or not:

- Who will they be with? Do you know these friends? Do you know their parents?
- Where will they be? Have you been there? Is it a safe place for them?
- When are they going? When will they be back?
- What will they be doing? Is it an appropriate activity for their age?
- Why do they want to go? Is it because they really want to, or are they being pressured by peers?

As we consider these questions, we realize that they are not only for our children to answer. Our ongoing involvement with our children has set the groundwork for making informed decisions. Independence needs to come gradually. When our children are preteens, we need to play a more direct role in monitoring their activities with friends. Dropping them off at the movies and/or picking them up is one example. Asking our children to call or text us, or texting them to check in is another example. As our children become teens and have demonstrated the ability to make responsible decisions, we can begin to give them more independence.

When deciding whether or not to give our permission, we can be guided by our values; the who, what, where, when, why questions; what we know about our children; and what we know about their friends. If we are on the borderline, will monitoring the outing by participating to a limited degree help?

As we consider our decision, we should be in conversation with our children. If we determine it's a go, there is still more to do. We need to discuss what can happen on this outing and what risks may be involved. What are the options, should things go wrong? We need to agree on behavior expectations. Very importantly, we need to set a firm time expectation for returning home. With our children, we also need to negotiate consequences that will take place if negative behavior occurs or if the curfew is not met. The consequences need to be something we will definitely follow through on with our teens. Determining the consequence ahead of time is key because if we wait to determine a consequence or "punishment" after something has gone wrong, it will be an emotional reaction. Grounding someone for six months because we were angry would be difficult to follow through on and would likely be an unfair consequence.

If we have had these preparatory conversations, we can trust that our teens will be prepared to be safe and responsible while enjoying their experiences. My daughter loves to recall the beaming face of my granddaughter after her first outing on her own. We build confidence in our children when they can successfully navigate the world without us.

Our children, like us, will sometimes make mistakes. Making those mistakes, while they are still under our watchful eye, will help them learn to make better decisions next time. Sometimes, after much consideration, the answer to their request will be no. Our children deserve to know why the answer is no. Perhaps at some point we will reconsider it. In any case, sharing our reasons will help them understand how to make good choices in the future. Our preteens and teens need to learn independence. Our efforts in guiding them to make responsible decisions will pay off as they become adults.

Helping Our Children Overcome Family Conflicts

When families model healthy living, their children learn how to care for themselves and become resilient when encountering difficult challenges. The behaviors and values that we share with our families provide guidance to our children in their formative and impressionable years of development. Use the following strategies to help your children become resilient when resolving conflicts and during times of uncertainty:

- Provide your children with daily quality time and the opportunity to hug and cuddle during the day's events.
- Set the family dinner time to accommodate all family members if possible. Due to long work days, some families have their children eat dinner at an earlier time. Children can enjoy a healthy snack when their parents eat dinner. During this time, engage in discussions; listen to your children with care as they describe their inner-most fears, successes, and challenges.
- Make time to play as a family. Family recreation relieves stress and provides a respite in which families can function in a healthy and positive environment.
- Plan a nightly bedtime routine for each child that allows time for individual daily reflection with a parent and reading a bedtime story. Plan a family vacation each year. The vacation can be camping for a couple of days at a local park if time and resources are limited. The vacation planning, participating, and memories will stay with your children forever.
- Talk with your children about fears as they arise. Reassure them that you are there to help them and advocate for their needs.
- Limit the amount of time that your child spends on electronic entertainment devices and television. These technological

15

wonders can be overly stimulating. Monitor their internet sites. A child's video game may have links to disturbing or adult content.

- Ensure your child has quiet time in the last hour before bedtime.
- Model empathy and care for your neighbors and community. Participate in community service with your family.
- Provide moral and ethical guidance to your children.

CHAPTER 3
SEEK SUPPORT
FROM YOUR EXTENDED FAMILY

Grandparents and other significant adults can have a huge impact on their grandchildren and children. Some grandparents are the primary caregivers for their grandchildren because their parents cannot adequately care for their children. Many grandmas and grandpas provide daily or multi-day care for their grandchildren each week. These grandparents provide significant infant and preschool care. Many grandparents also pick up their grandchildren from school and provide them with extended enrichment activities. Besides infant and preschool care, some of my favorite afterschool activities with my grandchildren include:

- Talking to them about life's transitions, how to cope with problems, and how to maintain a healthy outlook on life.
- Discussing future plans for career options and what it takes to prepare for and succeed in a particular career.
- Making cookies, cooking dinner together, and having fun in the kitchen.
- Sharing arts and crafts activities together that include making greeting cards, creating seasonal decorations, and painting together.
- Participating in outside adventures including hiking, sports, playing at the park, gardening, or playing in the water.

- Completing community service projects together. These include helping in the homeless shelter, planting trees, cleaning parks, or making gifts for seniors.
- Reading books, writing stories, and creating books with illustrations.
- Playing games and creating new ways to play card games.
- Learning more about the family history and researching the family's homeland and customs.
- Going to a museum, a historical monument, or participating in a nature outing.

I am impressed with how simple daily pleasures can help my grandchildren learn about their world. Frequently, I hear them use my very words to describe outings. My grandchildren can transform a simple activity into one of life's great adventures.

Add Multigenerational Play with Your Extended Families

For many of us, holiday gatherings include three or four generations of family members. What better way to bring family together than through multigenerational play? After a recent dinner, our family decided to play Heads Up. We took turns putting the cell phone up to our foreheads. On the phone was the word that the person holding the phone had to guess. The rest of us gave either verbal or nonverbal clues until the person either guessed or time ran out. We do not know if we were playing correctly, but we have never laughed so much.

The children participated enthusiastically as they watched their grandmother, uncles and aunts being silly. It was a joyful and unifying experience.

During family gatherings, people are happy to be together, but often, especially with children, conversations get stale. After a while, you run out of questions to ask. When we play a game together, our relationships are rejuvenated. We get to know each other better. We get closer. Then, we have more to talk about.

I've always felt that family is very important. Our children feel more secure when they feel encircled by people who love them. When we play as a family, we show we care and want to spend time with our children. Our children feel a sense of belonging. Some of the games we have played are various versions of Monopoly, Uno, Pictionary, and Jenga.

Organize Family Reunions

Each year our family plans various family reunions to relive the memories of family fun and to reconnect with our loved ones. The most basic family reunion includes a potluck dinner of favorite dishes that the family can share with new family members. Typically, we bring some of our children or grandchildren to these events so that our extended family can be acquainted with our newest family members.

At one memorable event, a future son-in-law asked my husband for permission to marry our daughter. At another, a son-in-law was introduced to our extended family. We regularly use the reunions to introduce new grandchildren to the relatives. Most recently, our ten month old twin granddaughters were the celebrities of the reunion. One granddaughter warmly greeted the relatives and was happily held by many. The other only wanted to be held by grandpa and wailed each time a new relative was introduced.

Many times, relatives will bring culturally relevant recipes that have been shared throughout the years at holiday dinners. My grandmother would make a German carrot vegetable casserole that was very flavorful. Another family member would bring a selection of appetizers that were made with care. One cousin specialized in making platters of delectable desserts that included home-made pies, cakes, brownies, and cookies. A son-in-law made his spicy tortilla dip while another cousin barbecued spicy chicken, ribs, and salmon. A newer attraction has been a taco bar that includes many spicy toppings. As the children and family share their recipes, family members reminisce on how favorite family recipes evolved over time.

Another tradition in these events is the sharing of photos and documents from times past. Typically, various family members bring a selection of items that have been in storage for years. They share these artifacts with the family to recall the history of the family. A couple of weeks ago, my cousin shared a letter that my dad had written to her grandmother over fifty years ago about a mission to which they were both donating funds. Each family member added another memory about this project. The discussion included fond memories of how each family member worked together on this project.

I enjoy scrapbooking and have created several books that document various generations of my family. Our family loves looking at these books at reunions while the older members share the history of various celebrations and events. I taped my great aunt, who was the oldest of our family clan at the time, as she told us stories about the grandfather that I never met. My grandchildren love looking at the individual personal growth books that I have created for each child. They also give me their art creations and school work samples which I integrate with photos in these books. Several times a year, I journal developmental milestones for each grandchild documenting their favorite activities. They also dictate stories to me that are included in these books. I plan to give the grandchildren their milestone books when they settle into their homes as young adults. One daughter plans on keeping her children's books as opportunities to reminisce at future family gatherings.

The most important outcomes of our family reunions are to connect us to our heritage. My grandchildren are excited that they have family members from many different cultures. The children are excited to learn a few basic words in different languages that add depth to these events. We typically incorporate diverse art projects and music at our family gatherings.

Occasionally, we travel to visit family members. During these trips, we integrate visiting historical sites while visiting family members. For example, we took our daughter to the various Smithsonian museums when visiting family in Washington DC. When visiting my family in Massachusetts, I took my younger cousin to the Salem

Witch Museum after we had read articles about this museum at the library. Our adventure was enhanced because we had read about what we would see and then could select activities that would expand the research we had conducted at the library.

Some family reunions include camping trips. At these events, we each take charge of certain meals and share our camping survival skills with our extended family. We recently introduced our family to a hobo stew that includes a mixture of ground beef patties topped with carrots, onions, assorted vegetables, seasoned with spices, and tightly wrapped in aluminum foil. The foiled packets are placed over hot coals in a campfire until fully cooked. Another family member prepared a fry pan casserole of vegetables and meat. Our nephew prepared an elaborate barbecue of ribs and chicken. Our grandkids are excited to meet their cousins and enjoy sharing activities such as swimming, hiking, playing in creeks, and running with a family dog.

Some of us provide art and crafts projects for the children that include beading, drawing, coloring, and constructing nature mobiles. The children are invited to participate in a family karaoke at night and share ghost stories while eating toasted s'mores around a campfire.

Our family agrees that these trips are more interesting and stimulating with our extended family. As we travel to these outings, we stop at funky and fun tourist points of interest and participate in local activities that capture the area's nature and history. We keep journals of our travels and collect postcards of memorable outings.

Create Camp Grandma Experiences

When my children were growing up, many of their friends vacationed at their grandparents' homes for a week to play and explore new adventures with their grandparents. When they returned from these mini vacations, they would rave for days about the many adventures they encountered on these treasured trips. Although my children did not have grandparents who traveled with their grandchildren, they were fortunate to share similar experiences with their friends' families. My children loved the opportunity to live a different life with a new family for several days. Once in high school, each daughter had a chance to live in Europe for several weeks during one summer with a different family. One daughter helped a family friend take care of their children in France. Another daughter was able to replicate this experience by participating as a Rotary Club Ambassador in Finland. Both of our daughters returned from this extended travel with more self-determination skills and confidence, as they each had encountered another country with a different language and lived with another family. Both successfully overcame many challenges on their own with our loving encouragement by phone.

When I became a grandparent, I was determined to create a Camp Grandma experience for our grandchildren. We would convene a family meeting with our grandchildren on where we would take our vacation and plan our play activities. All participating grandchildren had to be at least age three and be prepared to challenge themselves in becoming more independent with their older cousins or siblings. We have had five Camp Grandmas to date and all have survived and relished the experiences of becoming junior rangers at a state park, surviving beach board walk carnival rides, and taking day trips biking, hiking, and exploring parks. The favorite trip to date has been staying at the beach for several days. The grandchildren enjoy exploring nature, surviving wild carnival rides, playing in the tide pools and ocean, swimming in a pool, sharing ice cream cone eating with their cousins, and eating out at a variety of restaurants.

The grandkids earn allowances for maintaining their belongings, taking care of younger siblings and cousins, and tutoring each other on the intricacies of building a Lego village, math facts, reading readiness, social study explorations, and science experimentations. At the end of the trip they each receive a token allowance with which they can select journal postcards to add to their collection of drawings and stories about their trip. Once the children are returned to their parents, they relive their adventures for weeks by telling their stories of achievements to their parents and to anyone else who will listen to them. After our recent trip to the Santa Cruz Beach boardwalk for four days, my younger grandson raved about living in a hotel, as this was a new adventure that he loved. My granddaughter was finally tall enough to take a ride with grandpa on the Big Dipper roller coaster. The older grandson raved about the gourmet seafood platter he fully consumed at a fancy restaurant that was ordered from the adult menu!

Now that we have completed five Camp Grandma vacations, the grandkids are starting to talk about the family traditions that they are establishing with us on these great adventures. So far, the beach vacation has won as the ideal vacation destination for three out of five years. The kids rave about their walk to the ice cream shop with their cousins at night. They brag about staying out until it is dark at the boardwalk to see the bright lights of the carnival rides. These adventures will stay with them throughout their lives until they become parents themselves some day and initiate new family traditions. I feel fortunate that I am young enough as a grandma to share in these exuberant adventures. I am also mature enough that I can safely deliver the grandchildren back to their parents so that I can rest up for the next great adventure in grandparenting.

CHAPTER 4
PARTNER WITH YOUR CHILDREN'S SCHOOLS

Parents must evaluate their children's academic needs for school placement each school year. When identifying an appropriate school placement for your child, consider the following:

- Accurately assess your child's skill set. Consider how your child performs academically, socially, and emotionally. Check with your child's current teacher to obtain valuable input through a behavioral rating scale, at a teacher conference, or with anecdotal evidence.
- At the parent-teacher conference, ask questions about your child's performance that include:
  - How are the child's verbal, gross motor, fine motor and social skills relative to their classmates?
  - Does your child prefer to play alone?
  - Is your child resistant to participating in certain activities such as circle time while at school?
  - Is your child younger than others, and therefore likely to benefit from an additional year of preschool?
- Consider your child's temperament. A child who prefers structure will benefit from a smaller, quieter and more predictable environment. A child who has a lot of energy and enjoys sports might do better in a less academic and more physically active placement.

- Consider your own personal needs. With so many demands from work and home, it is important to keep things simple. Advantages of a neighborhood school include reduced driving and time commitments. A neighborhood school leads to a greater likelihood of forming a carpool. Parents who are relaxed are more available to engage in their child's current interests, to visit or volunteer at school, and to help build a community with other children and parents.
- Seek input from outside professionals. Consult your child's pediatrician if you or the current teacher suspect something is out of the norm such as a behavioral issue. Focus your attention to pinpoint your child's strengths and weaknesses and identify resources for additional support.
- Advocate for your child. You and your spouse know your child better than anyone else. Advocate for collecting as much information as you can to make an informed placement decision. Support services can be added as priorities may shift. It is important to be creative and resourceful to meet your child's needs. Mine the treasures that your child will bring into your lives.
- Do your homework. Visit the school with your child. Talk to parents of other students at the school. Factor in the cost of a school, as not all schools cost the same. Prioritize what is most important to you and your child, even as you recognize that no decision can be perfect.

Transition in the First Weeks of School

Many schools now begin in mid-August catching those of us, lulled by the lure of free time, sleeping late, and spontaneous visits with family and friends, by surprise. All of a sudden, it is necessary to mobilize our children and get them out the door early with their lunches, homework, backpacks, and freshly brushed hair. How can we best smooth this transition?

The prospect of a fresh start to the school year is marketed through back to school shopping for new outfits, school supplies, and backpacks. The prospect of reconnecting with friends, sharing summer experiences, and finding the new classroom are also helpful.

How can we best sustain this energy and enthusiasm beyond the first day?

One of my sons had a sixth grade teacher whose mission that first week was to hit the ground running in terms of organization and parental involvement. Each day my son brought home a checklist for us to review, initial, and then sign for him to bring to school the next morning. My son earned points for having all of his homework completed, his notebook organized etc. He lost points for loose papers, and notably the absence of a make or break parental signature page. At the end of the week, if he was successful in attaining the required number of points, my son would participate in the class party. The substance of the party varied and could include free time, a class outing, or watching an educational video.

On the other hand, those students who did not meet the required point minimum would have to stay after school, miss lunch, and most importantly go to another room during the reward time. This regime was harsh. Typically, the same students continuously missed out. From my educator's perspective, they often had learning disabilities such as attention deficit or executive functioning challenges. Yet in our own household this regime shaped a renewed commitment to organization.

Before going to sleep, under my watchful eye, my son packed his backpack according to his check sheet specifications. He placed it next to the exit door, where we could not possibly avoid it. The required parental signature document was taped on the front door next to the doorknob, for reference early the next morning. The ensuing day's outfit including shoes and socks were selected and laid out the night before. His lunch was prepared and labeled with his name and placed at the front of the shelf, eye level in the refrigerator. We didn't dare forget the lunch, as we were strongly discouraged from bringing it up to school if it were left behind.

This entire regime was an anathema to our somewhat chaotic style of parenting. It seemed both harsh and inflexible. Each morning, I found that my son was positioning at the starting line and sprinting to the car. Yet he learned the following valuable lessons:

- Figure out the new teacher's system.
- Like it or not, follow these instructions as the teacher is in charge.
- As much as possible, plan ahead and assemble the necessary items in advance.
- No matter what, bring the freshly minted parental signature sheet every day.

Become an Active Partner

Taking on the role of partner with our children's school is the best way to ensure our children will receive the best education possible. Research has shown a connection between parent engagement and improved student learning. This can be accomplished by the following suggestions:

- Know your children's teachers and the principal. Communicate regularly.
- Get to know various teachers' personalities and how they work with children. Learn about their expectations and goals for their students.
- Build two-way relationships with your children's teachers. Tell them about your family's values and traditions.
- Learn about what your children are learning. Some teachers send notes home with that information. If they do not, ask your children and ask the teachers. Look at the work your children bring home to get a clue. Sometimes schools hold literacy, math or science nights. These are great opportunities to become familiar with what and how your children are learning.
- Talk to your children about their day. If the answer you receive to "What did you learn?" is "Nothing," ask more specific questions. "Tell me something funny that happened in school today." "Tell me something surprising that happened." "Tell me something serious or sad that happened." These starters should get a conversation going.
- If your young child is having problems with homework or with schoolwork, and you are at a loss as to how to provide support, schedule a meeting with the teacher. Use the time to

share about your child's experience from your perspective and seek to understand what your child needs to be able to do from the teacher's perspective. At the end, clarify how the teacher will support your child's growth and how you will support it from home. Follow up until you are satisfied that your child is doing better.

- As children get older they should be encouraged to communicate directly with the teacher when they are having problems learning. It is also helpful to your child if you monitor to make sure the support is being sought and received.
- Help in the classroom or take part in classroom activities such as field trips to the extent you can. Children love seeing their parents at school. That will likely change when they reach middle school, so take advantage while you can.
- Get involved in school activities. Attend meetings and social events to keep abreast of the needs of the school at large. Parents can play a critical role in the school's welfare, whether through school beautification activities or fundraising efforts aimed at enhancing educational opportunities for students.
- Know that the school belongs to you as a member of the community. Own it. As you take on the feeling of ownership, so will your child. When children have a feeling of belonging in their school, they learn better.
- If English is not your first language and you are having trouble communicating at school, request a translator. Schools must provide translators when a language is spoken by at least fifteen percent of students at the school.

Establish Good Study Skills

Parents want academic success for their children. They know that a good education can open many doors of opportunity for them. Children, however, live in the here and now. They don't consider the long-term consequences of their decisions. How can we break down the lofty task of educating our children into doable tasks they can embrace? Here are five tips of actions that parents and children can do daily to establish good study habits:

- Do homework daily. Establish the habit of study by setting aside time for homework each day.
- Read every day. Whether it's part of the homework assignment or not, have your children read to you, with you, or alone every day.
- Allow your children to do their own homework; don't do it for them. If, after you have provided support, your children still commit errors, leave the errors. The teachers need to see what your children are doing wrong in order to know what they still need to teach.
- Teach children to work independently. They should read the instructions for the various homework assignments by themselves, and explain to you what they need to do. Support by asking questions rather than by telling them what to do.
- When your children are having problems with learning, motivate them. Along with making sure that the teachers provide support in the classroom, help your children understand that none of us is perfect.

Sometimes learning is hard and takes time, but your children can form good study habits. Strong study habits are formed through repetition. Even though each child is a creature of the moment, you can set the foundation for academic success one day at a time.

How to Access Community Resources for Your Child

What can parents do when they do not know what is bothering their child? In a recent case study, we met Joey's parents who complained that their son no longer wanted to go to kindergarten because he did not have friends. He suddenly developed stomach aches. This was not the first time that Joey complained. It was becoming a weekly and sometimes daily event. We provided Joey's parents with the following action plan:

- Talk with Joey to determine how he was feeling about the challenges at school. Find out if there were children bothering him. Try to determine if he was creating the conflicts with his classmates. Ask Joey if the schoolwork was bothering him. Question if something at home was upsetting him. Brainstorm solutions for resolving some of the conflicts as school.

- Meet with the teacher to find out what was going on at school. For example, was Joey being too aggressive with his classmates? Did he have trouble focusing on classwork? Was Joey bored with the assignments and did he need more stimulation?

- After meeting with the teacher, mom might need to meet with her physician to identify any health-related issues that can be contributing to Joey's anxieties and stomach aches.

- When meeting with the doctor, mom may want to request a referral for a family therapist that can help her assist Joey in reducing extreme and recurring anxieties at school.

- Mom can also receive referrals for family support through the school, at community social service agencies, and by asking friends for their contacts for help. Sometimes, anxiety issues come from changes in the home. Other times, children can be a victim of bullying.

- Occasionally, the problem may be an indication of a learning disability that has not been previously identified. If there is a potential learning disability, the school will ask for the parents' permission to evaluate the child for further special education services. Parents can also seek outside support and obtain referrals from community-based agencies. Parents Helping Parents provides extensive information and referral services for families of children with special needs.

As Joey's mom further investigated his fear of school, she soon learned that Joey was reacting to typical stresses of being a big brother to a new baby sister. When meeting with his teacher, mom learned that she could give Joey more encouragement and autonomy in the home as a big brother and helper with his new baby sister. Mom arranged for Joey to have play dates with classmates. Joey's mom also scheduled special times for quality time with mom or dad. His teacher addressed Joey's need for attention and coping by giving him added encouragement and responsibilities at the school.

Today, Joey is in first grade. He is happy to be at school. Joey has many friends and he brings them home for afterschool play dates. He is performing well academically. Most of the time he is happy to be a big brother. Joey is a leader and loves to show his baby sister how to play with his big boy toys.

Support Your Child's Academic Struggles

Teachers and principals work with a multitude of children each day. Often children have similar problems. It becomes convenient to sometimes define a student by his or her problem rather than see the student as a complete, unique human being. Parents know their children better than anyone else. In a problem-solving situation, parents can bring this perspective to the table. When children have difficulty in school, parents bring the knowledge of who the child is; how the child feels; and how the actions the school may take will impact him or her. This important perspective will help develop solutions that are more likely to work for the individual child.

I know a parent whose child was having behavior problems at school. The teacher was dealing with the child's behavior by using her progressive discipline chart. The child's behavior "progressed" to the lowest level of performance on the chart. In addition, the child was getting into confrontations in the school yard. Finally, the principal called the child into the office and requested that mom come to meet with her. When the child's mother arrived, the child was very hostile to both his mother and the principal. Mom and the principal agreed that the child would be placed on in-house suspension on the subsequent Monday.

While the child was cooling off in another room, mom and the principal discussed what had been happening in the child's life up to that time. Mom described that her child was feeling discouraged in various aspects of his life. The progressive downward trend in his behavior in the classroom was making him feel that he could never be a good student. Mom and the principal concluded that they needed to implement consequences that would encourage rather than further discourage this child. They discussed actions that would be taken at home and at school to help the child work successfully. The solutions included a referral to a counselor.

Over the weekend mom and the child worked together to accomplish tasks at home. His contributions were recognized with positive feedback. Those tasks included school work that needed to be caught up. On Monday, part of the in-house suspension time was used for a meeting between the child and the principal to make behavioral plans that included options on how to behave in difficult situations. The child would be checking in with the principal to assess his continuing progress. Things have greatly improved for the child and continue to progress for the better.

Every child can be successful in school. Problems must be addressed, but to be addressed effectively, parents need to be part of the solution. They bring the perspective of the whole child to the problem-solving process. It can be the difference between success and failure.

Participate in the School's Community Service Days

I just participated in a community service day at my grandchildren's school. It was an evening of fun that included the following activities for children and their families:

- Making cards for seniors
- Creating dog toys
- Decorating blankets
- Making community garden decorations
- Collecting clothes, books, and toys

My grandchildren loved making the dog toys. I had fun creating a greeting card for a senior and having my grandson teach me how to draw winter plants and decorations. The highlight of my day was watching my grandchildren learn with their friends. They learned more about those who do not have family and friends living nearby to care for them. My learning from this event includes the following:

- My grandchildren and their friends learned about the various types of community members that need help in their city.
- The children learned about products and services that can provide added comfort to these community members.

- Children can offer love and respect to their neighbors by sharing their art projects and greeting cards.
- The products made by the children will provide seniors and others with the knowledge that their community loves them.
- Children can support community services throughout the year.
- Families can join together as a school community and help those in need on a regular basis.

A school's community service days can teach children how their service can support their neighbors who need added care.

CHAPTER 5
ORGANIZE FAMILY PLAY

When a family embraces its values and sets clear expectations, children can be confident about what is important in their daily lives. Additionally, a family can use its values to determine how it will spend its time together and plan for its future. A family can identify its values through the following activity:

- Convene a family meeting about members' expectations for your daily life with each other.
- Have family members share what they think are important expectations or values for your family.
- Make a list of all identified values, vote on four, and select those with the most votes.
- Create a family shield, crest, or symbol to represent your family's values.
- List the four top values in an artistic representation and frame or post in a prominent location in your home.

For example, a family created a heart symbol to illustrate their following family values:

- Family is important.
- Each family member is caring and respectful of individual differences.

- The family gives back to their community through service activities.
- The family values education and learning.

Finally, the heart of the family's values was posted on the refrigerator. Family members reviewed it when they struggled with being able to set priorities in their daily lives.

Review your list of values with your family each week during meal time. Embrace your family's values in your actions, words, and family play. Consider adding or changing values over time as your family grows.

How to Create Family Projects that Help Your Child Learn

As parents, we constantly are challenged as to how and when to support our children's learning at home. We have learned from teachers that children learn best when they are given the chance to explore academic experiences at their own pace through project-based learning experiences. Within the classroom, a teacher strives to create a holistic learning environment that can adequately support the social-emotional, cognitive, and physical development of each child. At home, we can enhance our children's daily activities by allowing our children to explore and create at their own level of understanding with projects that facilitate learning.

For example, a preschooler, an elementary age child, a middle school child and their dad recently created a container vegetable garden. The project included the following primary activities:

- Research how to construct container gardens on the internet and in gardening books. Determine how much wood, nails, and other construction supplies will be needed to construct the container. Measure the area that will be covered by the container. Determine how deep the container should be for proper vegetable growth and irrigation.
- Once the container supplies have been purchased, construct the container.

- Determine how much dirt must be purchased for filling the newly constructed container and pour it into the container.
- Identify the various vegetables that will grow best in a specific season and purchase the seeds. Plant the seeds according to the instructions for each type of vegetable.
- Construct netting or other types of protection over the garden to ensure insects and animals cannot harvest the crops too soon.
- Water each vegetable plant and fertilize as needed to ensure healthy growth.
- Harvest crops as they mature. Plan meals that include the use of various vegetables from the garden. Create recipes that will include the harvested crops.

When we include our children in the planning and development of a container vegetable garden, the children can learn and explore the project-based learning at their own pace. The preschooler will be happy to help dad construct parts of the container, shovel dirt into the container, plant larger vegetable seeds, sprinkle the vegetables with water, and help harvest and cook with the crops. The elementary age child could also help dad calculate the various amounts of materials that would be required for the construction of the container, the amount of soil required, and how many vegetables of each type could be planted in the container. The middle school child could additionally research the project's cost and help dad work within a specific budget. All three children, at these various levels of project-based learning, can benefit in their overall academic learning in language arts, math, science, and social studies. Added language arts and performing arts activities for all ages could include keeping a daily journal with illustrations on the growth of the various vegetables when considering changing weather patterns. All of the children could compare the growth of different types of vegetable plants to determine which plants grow best in their yard. Added research could be conducted on the use of various amounts of water and the impact on the growth of plants. Environmental conditions can also be researched on the internet to determine how to manage soil conditions, insect infestations, drought conditions, and other variables that can impact the healthy growth of the plants.

This one home project of growing a garden can expand each child's social-emotional growth by nurturing their creativity and responsible behaviors in managing their role in developing and maintaining the family garden. Children can cognitively grow in this experience at their own level of interest and academic understanding. Each child can also participate in the outside activity that will build strength and endurance with the construction of the garden and the ongoing maintenance of the garden. Finally, the children will take pride in creating healthy recipes for the family that will include the use of all vegetables. Typically, children who create or grow something will be more prone to eating it. They will also take pride in helping others appreciate their produce. When children learn to eat healthy meals at an early age, they tend to reinforce these healthy behaviors throughout life.

Our project-based learning example of growing a family garden may seem simplistic, but it can have a lasting impact on the family. Each evening, the family members can harvest the crops for a salad, discuss how each vegetable is growing while eating dinner, and determine how they can prepare new recipes that are healthy when using a variety of vegetables from the garden. If a family lives in an apartment that does not have garden space, many cities have community gardens that families can share and develop into vegetable gardens. Additionally, many seniors would be happy to have young families help them develop a shared garden in their yard. Families with younger children would also love to share in a family garden with older children in their neighborhood.

Have Your Children Grocery Shop and Prepare Meals

Parents can have a wonderful time grocery shopping with your children and helping them select appropriate groceries for meal planning. My older grandchildren review the nutritional value of a couple of food items and compare the fat content, amount of sodium, and other unhealthy ingredients. We also conduct a price analysis to determine the best value for the price. We discuss which product tastes the best or will produce the greatest satisfaction as this is an important factor to consider when comparison shopping. When purchasing produce, my grandchildren note the cost per pound of a specific vegetable or fruit. They will then weigh each type of fruit or vegetable and calculate the approximate cost for each. After the food is purchased, the grandchildren can compare the final cost to their projected cost of various produce items. We enhance our grocery shopping experiences by:

- Planning meals
- Preparing a shopping list for specific meals
- Cooking the meals while discussing fractional conversions for recipes

As a child becomes experienced in grocery shopping, he or she can walk through the store to search and select specific food items to buy. Middle school students can create the weekly family shopping list and then shop for the family when using a predetermined budget. This was actually my weekly chore when I was a middle school student. This activity prepared me for nutritional meal planning while using a fixed food budget. It reinforced my literacy and math skills. I also learned about the sociological impact of food displays in stores while shopping with various cultural groups. I used science to evaluate healthy food choices and modify family recipes based on available seasonal produce.

Plan Summer Activities with Your Children

Summer offers a wide range of activities for kids: both educational and recreational. Each comes with a price tag in dollars, in time, and in the alternatives we give up. It is important to weigh these various costs and benefits by considering the following:

- In making a choice of summer school or camp, it is important to get your children's input. They are the ones who will be participating. Have your children make a list of all the positives and negatives for competing choices. Examples of some of the questions they should consider include:
  o Do I have any friends going?
  o How difficult is it for me to wake up early in the morning?
  o Do I enjoy being outside?

- o Will I get bored by the same activity all day?
- o How much do I enjoy learning new things?
- Compile your own pro-con list. It may be helpful to encourage your children to choose only one sport, select a school that is close by, or find an afternoon activity that will allow you to drop off your child during lunch and pick them up after work. If your children will take summer school, help them choose classes with other benefits. For example, get your child a prep period during the high school year by satisfying a requirement during the summer. Ultimately, it is important to evaluate what is manageable financially and time wise for you as a parent. It is important that the choice of a summer activity be the outcome of a careful discussion with input from your children rather than what you might hear about at the little league field.
- Summer should be a time for rest and rejuvenation, exploring something new and creative play. There will never be any perfect choice. Rather, think of summer as a time for your children to practice decision-making, to explore their hearts and ignite their interests. Other questions to consider include:
  - o Are any of these activities only offered in the summer?
  - o What is the refund policy for cancellation?
  - o How might these activities enhance my children's self-esteem?

I would like to conclude with an example from one of my student's experiences. John (a sophomore in high school with auditory memory problems and ADHD) needed to fill in one more class during his second semester. Due to a failing grade, John had to drop the second semester of geometry. The only class available that would fulfill his requirements was ceramics. As an added bonus, at his high-school, glass blowing was included in ceramics. For the next two years in high school, John went on to become a teacher's aide in glass blowing; leading to paid work in the summer. Best of all, John won a scholarship to study glass blowing at a post-secondary school in Italy. Our teaching staff would never have predicted that John's decision to take ceramics would lead to this life-long passion and occupation. Analysis of various decisions need not lead to paralysis.

CHAPTER 6
CHERISH YOUR CAPABLE CHILDREN

When parents have implemented the *Effective Parenting! Capable Kids!* strategies included in the book, we have received reports that children are happier, more productive, and more capable in their homes, classrooms and communities. Children need their parents to role model how they can become capable and responsible contributors to the daily needs of their home and prepared students in the classroom. When kids feel confident about their contributions in the home and school, they become resilient when overcoming daily challenges. When parents model strong communication and conflict resolution skills, their children are able to adapt these skills in their own interactions with other adults, teachers, and friends. Parents who seek added support from family and friends help children become more independent as their children learn to work with other adults successfully. When parents partner with their children's schools, the kids are confident that their activities at school are important to their parents. Added family play and community service activities help children learn the value of contributing leadership skills within their families and communities.

When considering the concepts and case studies shared in the book, complete the action plan and family value chart in this chapter to help you and your children increase your skills and activities in building effective parenting practices to support capable kids. Share your success stories with us at GenParenting.com or at hello@genparenting.com. May your family's journey to success be filled with many satisfying adventures!

Our Action Plan to Achieve *Effective Parenting! Capable Kids!*

Strategy	Current Successful Strategy	Opportunity for Growth
Communication		
Conflict Resolution		
Extended Family		
Partnering with Schools		
Family Play		

**Embrace Your Family's Values
to Support Effective Parents and Capable Kids**

Families can identify their goals by convening a family meeting.

Each family member can share what they value about their family.

The family can select four values that best represent their family's daily activities and create a list of these values below:

Our Shared Family Values

1. _____

2. _____

3. _____

4. _____

When families set clear expectations and values, children are confident about what is important in their daily lives.

Review the list with family members regularly and embrace your values in your actions and work.

RELATED BOOKS AND RESOURCES

Active Parenting of Teens by Michael H. Popkin, published by Active Parenting in 2009

This book is a good resource for parents of preteens and teens. It provides parents with an understanding of adolescents' physical and emotional development, and strategies for effective communication and problem-solving. Parents learn what they can do to support their children through this critical time in their development.

Beyond the Bake Sale, The Essential Guide to Family-School Partnerships by Anne T. Henderson, Karen L. Mapp, Vivian R. Johnson and Don Davies, published by The New Press in 2007

This is a guide for developing meaningful home-school partnerships where power is shared by all stakeholders for the benefit of students. Various checklists are provided to guide the process covering topics such as bridging racial, class and cultural differences and evaluating school district support and community engagement.

Preparing Children for Success in School and Life by Marcia L. Tate, published by Corwin Press in 2011

As their children's first teachers, how can parents and caregivers play with their children to achieve to their fullest potential? This book provides parents with guidance on how to create a healthy home environment with love, verbal communication, creativity, and imaginative play that can guide children of all ages towards personal, academic, and career success.

The Art of Tinkering by Karen Wilkinson and Mike Petrich, published by Weldon Owen in 2013

This is a book of activities combining art, science, and technology written by the directors of the Exploratorium of San Francisco's Tinkering Lab. Tinkering encourages students of all ages to explore and experiment with various media, tools, and everyday objects to better understand how the world works. These activities encourage students to take things apart and create new things. Parents can engage with their children in these creative endeavors.

Tinkerlab, A Hands-On Guide for Little Inventors by Rachelle Doorley, published by Roost Books in 2014

This guide is full of projects that provide learning experiences for young children through play and creativity. Parents will be guided in creating inside and outside spaces for creativity at home. The focus of tinkering is in the process rather than in the outcome. Many opportunities for learning through creating are provided using a multitude of materials.

What If Everybody Understood Child Development? by Rae Pica, published by Corwin Press in 2015

What is the connection between how children grow and learn? This book provides a selection of real-life stories shared by teachers and parents with references, related articles, and interviews with experts. Parents will gain insight and understanding on how the Common Core Standards, the self-esteem movement, and standardized testing in schools can impact student learning and how parents can support their children's success.

ABOUT THE AUTHORS

Rosemarie Pérez has worked with English learners and their families in public education for more than twenty years. She has served as a bilingual teacher, professional developer, district administrator, and parent engagement expert. Administrative roles included serving as the Director of English Learners for an elementary school district and as a Coordinator of Reading and Language for the San Mateo County Office of Education. Rosemarie continues to work with families as she leads the Santa Clara County Office of Education's Parent Engagement Initiative during the past three years. Ms. Pérez provides expert guidance to teachers, school site staff, and school administrators in creating culturally sensitive parent training modules and academic curricular units. She facilitates parent education and Common Core Standards workshops. Engaged parents are further trained to become parent leaders and advocates. Rosemarie is the mother of five adult children and three grandchildren that include a thirteen year old granddaughter and ten year old twins. She currently lives with her niece and seven year old grandnephew.

Karen Salzer has over thirty years of experience as a resource teacher in the Palo Alto public schools. She earned a doctorate in education from Stanford University. Her areas of expertise involve working with culturally diverse students with special needs including autism, emotional disturbances, learning disabilities, and health issues. As a special educator, Ms. Salzer served as a liaison between parents of special needs students and school staff. She guided parents and staff in identifying an appropriate education for each student in the public school setting. Additionally, she aided students and parents in navigating the educational requirements for graduation, test-taking and in finding support services within the community. Through her leadership, Ms. Salzer encouraged collaborative problem-solving between parents and school staff – such as accommodations for test taking, extended time and use of technology. She loves to follow-up with her students when they become adults and to highlight their many successes in education and careers. Ms. Salzer uses these success testimonials to reassure parents of other children and to encourage them to help their children pursue their full potential. Ms.

Salzer is the mother of four adult children and helps care for an infant grandson, a toddler grandson, and a pre-kindergarten granddaughter.

Carole Flowers has over fifty years of nursing experiences with diverse students from preschool through high school. Carole served Oakland Unified School District as a nursing leader and administrator for twenty-nine years. Areas of expertise included assisting children with special education needs and families with high stress and disabilities. Ms. Flowers served as the district liaison with the Public Health Department, the Asthma Coalition, the HIV Curriculum Project, and the Task Force for Obesity in Schools. Carole also provided support services to pregnant teens, students with incarcerated parents, and children who were being raised by their grandparents or in foster group homes. Added community services were provided to students and their families who abused illegal drugs, alcohol, or prescription medications. Ms. Flowers continues to be instrumental in inspiring students and their families to develop resiliency and survival skills to overcome their life's circumstances. Carole is the mother of an adult daughter and a daughter who passed away from triple negative breast cancer at the age of forty. Ms. Flowers has formally and informally adopted hundreds of children in desperate need of loving support.

Mary Ann Burke has served as a credentialed parent educator and adjunct professor for over thirty years in California's schools. Dr. Burke has presented effective parenting and school engagement strategies at numerous state and national parent engagement events. She is the author of four Corwin Press Books on parent and community engagement in schools. Mary Ann Burke previously led the Santa Clara County Office of Education's Parent Engagement Initiative that serves as a state model for best practices in parent engagement for culturally diverse families. She creates Common Core State Standards kits for parents to use at home and in their child's classroom to support children's literacy and academic readiness skills. Mary Ann is an active grandmother of five grandchildren. She is active in her grandchildren's literacy and academic developmental activities. Mary Ann shares this expertise with various educators and school leaders as a trainer, author, and curriculum developer.

52122058R00032

Made in the USA
San Bernardino, CA
11 August 2017